Remembering
Atlanta

Michael Rose

Atlanta History Center

TURNER

PUBLISHING COMPANY

Crowds line Peachtree Street during the "Heroes Day" parade to celebrate the end of World War II. The city was an important military center during the war, with establishments at Fort McPherson, Camp Gordon, Lawson General Hospital, and the present Fort Gillem. Together with the local military industries and the city's traditional role as a transportation center, World War II transformed Atlanta into the South's unrivaled leading metropolitan area.

Remembering
Atlanta

Turner Publishing Company
www.turnerpublishing.com

Remembering Atlanta

Copyright © 2010 Turner Publishing Company

Library of Congress Control Number: 2010924319

ISBN: 978-1-59652-662-4

Printed in the United States of America

ISBN: 978-1-68336-807-6 (pbk.)

CONTENTS

Dr. and Mrs. Martin Luther King, Jr., and the Reverend and Mrs. Ralph David Abernathy tour Markham Street in one of the city's most impoverished areas in January 1966. Residents in the Vine City neighborhood were protesting poor housing conditions, which Dr. King deemed "a shame on the community." After Dr. King was awarded the Nobel Peace Prize in 1964, the city honored him with the first officially integrated dinner in the city's history.

ACKNOWLEDGMENTS

All of the photographs included in *Remembering Atlanta* are from the collection of the Kenan Research Center at the Atlanta History Center.

I would like to acknowledge the individuals and institutions who have generously donated photographs and acquisition funds to the Kenan Research Center and who have made possible the quality and quantity of visual collections that made this book possible.

Thanks, as always, to the staff of the Kenan Research Center for their advice, patience, and understanding. And thanks to Franklin M. Garrett, who led the way.

Above all, thanks go to Betsy Rix, for her understanding of graphic excellence, magic with digital imaging, unlimited patience and perseverance, and unfailing good humor.

—Michael Rose

PREFACE

A picture is worth a thousand words, as the saying goes. The idea being that a photograph in itself can express what may require many paragraphs of a book's text to explain. The images collected here offer a glimpse of time through Atlanta's history. Though not a history of the city, they are arranged chronologically from the earliest-known existing photograph taken in the city to those from the later twentieth century. Some images may be familiar, but the collection presented here provides many scenes of Atlanta never seen or never published before.

These photographs are both representational and symbolic. Some present street scenes or views of the city throughout time, others may provide a sense of time and place, evoking a feeling or sentiment from the viewer. Some images are iconic—many photographs of Dr. Martin Luther King, Jr., convey the concepts of justice and equality for which he stood, of the civil rights movement and the struggle for racial equality.

Photographers for many of the photographs are known, ranging from George N. Barnard, who traveled with General William T. Sherman's army, to modern photojournalists such as Kenneth G. Rogers, Bill Wilson, and Floyd Jillson of the city's large newspapers, or Boyd Lewis, who worked in Atlanta's counterculture alternative press. For a number of years, the images in the book are the work of professional studio photographers, and most of the building views and street scenes are commercial work executed by them. It is not until the early twentieth century that amateur photography appears, presenting Atlantans in informal poses, riding in cars, and smiling. As the twentieth century progresses, the photojournalism of professional news photographers appears as newspapers document a changing city.

Although the image presents the visual record, some words contain a visual legend that in them brings photographs and images to mind. Peachtree, Scarlett, and Sherman are three words that in many ways defined the public's perception of Atlanta for decades—a timeless reflection of Civil War Atlanta reinforced by the novel *Gone With the Wind*. Add to them Coca-Cola, CNN, Delta, and the Olympic Games, and the impression that comes to mind is the emerging Atlanta of the twentieth century—the home of the "Atlanta Spirit," in which business and promotion characterize the city.

Atlanta is a city of words and images, presented here to give the viewer a sketch of time, both distant and close. The city has lost much of its physical past—it is missing the first City Hall and all of the antebellum town, each of its four historic passenger train depots (all of them razed), as well as many of the homes and businesses that once lined the streets throughout the city. *Remembering Atlanta* remembers many of these places as well as the people who have lived, worked, and played in a city born in a southern forest, founded by a train engineer who one day drove a stake in the ground where he thought it should be.

Passengers wait on a flatboat on the Chattahoochee River at the Mayson-Turner Ferry, which crossed the river at the site of the present Bankhead Highway. Atlanta was situated for its rail lines and not for convenience to a main waterway. Nevertheless, ferry crossings along the Chattahoochee River supplied the city with historic street names, including Paces Ferry, Montgomery Ferry, Powers Ferry, and Johnson Ferry. Ironically, Atlanta's first ferry crossing was located at a site named Shallowford.

A Stake in the Wilderness: From Birth to Destruction

(1860–1864)

Like ferry crossings, the area's saw and grist mills provided place names throughout Atlanta, including Moores Mill, Howell Mill, Akers Mill, Terrell Mill, and Tilly Mill. In late August 1864, following a month-long siege of Atlanta, Union general William T. Sherman attempted to cut the city's railroad supply lines south of town. His victory on September 1 in the Battle of Jonesboro near Jester's Old Mill forced Confederate troops to finally evacuate Atlanta.

Unlike the plantation South where cotton was king, Atlanta's early economy was based on commerce and the railroads. Though the site of this house is unknown, photographer George N. Barnard noted its location as Atlanta. One of the area's largest antebellum plantations belonged to James H. Kirkpatrick, who moved to DeKalb County in 1827. At the time of his death in 1853, Kirkpatrick owned 1,000 acres, much of which was later developed into the Kirkwood neighborhood.

This street scene depicts the way much of antebellum Atlanta would have appeared—dirt roads and all. In 1860, the city was home to fewer than 10,000 residents. As the war evolved over the next few years, the population grew to nearly 22,000. This quiet city street would have been filled with Confederate soldiers and the citizens who worked in factories, hospitals, warehouses, and other war-related activities.

Completed in 1854, Atlanta's Passenger Depot sat at the very heart of the city near the Zero-Mile Post, designating the southern terminus of the Western & Atlantic Railroad. The depot served four rail lines that linked the Southeast, creating the transportation and manufacturing hub that would become General Sherman's target. The depot is seen from the first bridge to be built over the tracks, making it safer to cross from one side of the city to the other.

The large top hat on the right side of the street advertises J. M. Holbrook's store on Whitehall Street. Holbrook offered men's hats, caps, straw goods, and trunks, as well as canes and umbrellas. From early Atlanta to the mid twentieth century, Whitehall Street served as the city's central business district. As a result of its commercial importance, everything in this photograph was destroyed before the Union army's departure from Atlanta.

When completed in 1859, the home of John Neal was the height of antebellum splendor. All brick, with a majestic columned portico and surmounted by a standard for fashionable homes, a cupola. Neal's house stood at the corner of Washington and Mitchell streets, across the street from Atlanta City Hall, in one of the foremost residential sections of the city. For that reason, the house served as General Sherman's headquarters during the occupation.

This and the following two images are from a panorama of Atlanta, taken from the cupola of the Atlanta Female Institute by photographer George N. Barnard during the Federal occupation of the city, September-November 1864. This view presents the city from the Atlanta Medical College to the southeast (the domed building at upper-left) to residences along present Courtland Street. The female seminary was dismantled by Union troops, who used the bricks for winter shelters that went uninhabited that winter.

— CAR - SHED —

Though photographed during the war, this scene presents not only the look of antebellum Atlanta, but the appearance of this part of the city after Sherman left on the March to the Sea. All of the houses and outbuildings in this view remained, with the exception of the Passenger Depot (at the horizon, middle-left) and a few buildings in Atlanta's commercial district that are discernible in the distance.

After occupying Atlanta, Sherman ordered a line of fortifications in the event of a resurgent Confederate attack. The forts were constructed southeast of the city's center, creating a concentrated, compact defensive perimeter. Federal Fort No. 19 lay astride the rail line of the Georgia Railroad running east to Augusta. The scene looks northwest toward the city across the tracks; the cupola of the Atlanta Medical College rises just beyond the tree at left.

A fort along the Confederate line faces the present Georgia Tech campus from the site of the Administration Building. Part of Atlanta's defense was to clear timber for a distance of 1,000 yards in front of earthwork fortifications. In December 1864, a report on the area's destruction noted that "for miles around, scarcely a tree is standing." Faced with this landscape, Sherman laid siege to the city, bombarding Atlanta throughout the month of August.

Fort Hood, the northernmost redoubt in the city's defenses, overlooks fortifications erected on the property of planter and slave trader Ephraim G. Ponder. Ponder had moved to Atlanta in 1857, when he built the house in the distance on the edge of what is now the Georgia Tech campus. The house served as a Confederate sharpshooter's position until heavily shelled by Sherman's artillery, which was bombarding the city from the woods near present-day Eighth Street.

A Federal soldier sits atop the sand-bagged cannon redoubt of the captured Confederate Fort Hood overlooking the Marietta road. A line of rifle pits extends into the distance, screened by sharpened, interlocking logs called chevaux-de-frise. "It is astonishing to see what fortifications they had every side of the city," a Union soldier wrote from Atlanta. "All in vain for them," he concluded, "but quite convenient for us."

General William T. Sherman poses with his staff in Federal Fort No. 7, which had been the westernmost redoubt in the Confederate defensive line. The position stood on high ground located on the edge of the present Clark Atlanta University campus at the corner of Fair Street and the present Joseph E. Lowery Boulevard. Federal troops entered the city on September 3, 1864, and remained until departing for the March to the Sea on November 15.

In this view north on Washington Street, the house at left built by John Neal before the war was the home of state Supreme Court judge Richard F. Lyon by 1864. Beyond are the Second Baptist and Central Presbyterian churches, and the home of Atlanta's mayor, James M. Calhoun, in the distance. Calhoun surrendered the city to Union forces on the northern edge of the city's fortifications, near the Ponder house.

The facilities of the Western & Atlantic Railroad stood north of downtown Atlanta, near the present site of CNN headquarters. These buildings were left in ruins after Federal troops destroyed most of the city's transportation facilities in mid November 1864. "We have been utterly destroying everything in the city of any use to the armies of the South," an Indiana soldier wrote. "General Sherman is credited with saying 'War is Hell.' I think that it is."

The Crawford, Frazer & Company slave market was located at No. 8 Whitehall Street (now Peachtree Street), one block uphill from the rail line. Atlantan L. C. Butler remembered the benches surrounding the room on which slaves were seated. "Here," he said, "the prospective buyers made their selections just as they would have a horse or mule at a stockyard." The site of the slave market is now the entrance to the city's Five Point MARTA station.

This view looks down Alabama
Street from the corner of
Whitehall Street (now Peachtree
Street) toward the Georgia
Railroad locomotive house.
The area is now the heart of
Underground Atlanta. One of the
civilian casualties of Sherman's
bombardment, Solomon Luckie
was killed when he was struck
by shell fragments at this corner.
Luckie was one of the city's free
African Americans and ran a
barbershop and bathing salon at
the nearby Atlanta Hotel.

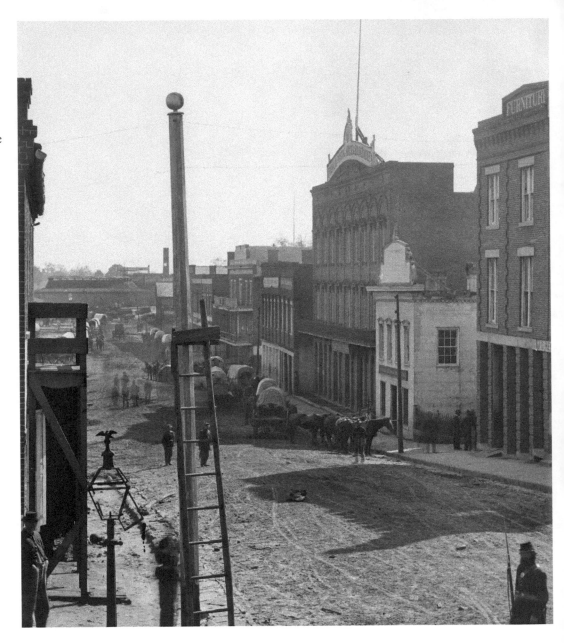

The Calico House was headquarters of Sherman's chief engineer, Captain Orlando M. Poe. Poe directed the destruction of Atlanta's commercial, military, and transportation infrastructure before the March to the Sea. Built for attorney Marcus Aurelius Bell in 1860, the house stood at the corner of present Auburn Avenue and Courtland Street. The residence was marbled in shades of blue, yellow, and red. Atlantans believed the simulated effect looked more like calico fabric than classic marble, thus the nickname.

Federal officers relax on the steps of the home of Er Lawshé, located on Peachtree Street between Cain and Harris streets. After the war, this house was requisitioned as headquarters for the commander of the Post of Atlanta, Prince Felix Salm-Salm, a brigadier general from Prussia. Though this was an imposing two-story residence with trellised and columned porches, the wife of the commander, Agnes Leclerq Salm-Salm, described it as "a very nice little cottage."

This house on Peachtree Street shows damage both under the roofline and to the chimney at right—probably from shelling during the Federal bombardment of the city during August. The siege was horrifying for residents of the city. Sherman himself wrote to Confederate general John B. Hood, criticizing him for defending the city "on a line so close to town that every cannon shot and many musket shots . . . went into the habitations of women and children."

Officers and troops of the Union Army of the Cumberland pose on the porch of a house located on what was known as "Upper" Peachtree Street, the section between Ellis and Butler streets. Major General George H. Thomas' headquarters was located in the Herring-Leyden House near the intersection of Ellis and Peachtree streets. Subsequently, many of the homes in the area were appropriated by officers of his army.

Federal troops dismantled and destroyed the city's railroad network in the last days of the Federal occupation of Atlanta in November 1864. The destruction of Atlanta's military capabilities had been Sherman's goal and the subsequent damage to surrounding homes and private property ruined a significant section of downtown Atlanta.

The center of Atlanta and the basis for its existence, the depot and rail lines had transformed a city in the forest into a major transportation and commercial center. Yet the Union Passenger Depot, commonly called the "Car Shed," lay in ruins when Sherman departed on the March to the Sea. "The devastation of the city was so widespread," a Union private wrote, "that I don't think any people will want to try and live there now."

The Phoenix Rises: From Ashes to New South Capital

(1865–1899)

Seen from the Broad Street Bridge, Union Station was completed in 1871. The Kimball House to the left opened in 1870. With 240 rooms, the hotel was painted yellow with brown trim and provided elevators and central heat. Rising six stories, it was considered by many Atlantans to be "too large for the community," and its builder, Hannibal Kimball, was in financial trouble before it was completed. Yet the hotel was a source of city pride until destroyed by fire in 1883.

In the 1870s, this fountain on Marietta Street provided public watering for horses. In early Atlanta, Walton Springs was located nearby in the vicinity of present Carnegie Way and Andrew Young International Boulevard. The area of the spring had been popular for strolling in antebellum Atlanta and became home to bombproofs dug into the hillsides during the war. Spring Street is named for the spring and Walton Street for its owner, Anderson W. Walton.

A horse-drawn trolley moves past hitching rails along the city's first length of street rails on Alabama Street. The cupola at the end of the street is the Georgia Railroad Freight Depot; the cupola at right is Atlanta City Hall. The small cupola at center-left is Fire Engine House No. 2, which like city hall survived Sherman's destruction. This section of Alabama is south of present Peachtree Street and part of Underground Atlanta.

The Tallulah Fire Company No. 3 was organized in February 1859 following the city's first fire-related deaths earlier that winter. The volunteer company adopted uniforms—orange jackets with black pants and red caps trimmed in blue, along with the motto "We Strive to Save." The company's brick firehouse stood on present Broad Street between Marietta and Walton streets. The city's all-volunteer fire companies served until the fire department was authorized in 1882.

The First Methodist Church appears at the end of the section of Peachtree Street running from the Luckie Street intersection to today's Margaret Mitchell Square. Atlanta's first church building was a one-room frame structure erected in 1847 near this site. Prior to that, Dr. William N. White noted that "not a church has yet been built . . . preaching is held in the railroad depot."

Carriages wait for passengers outside the station along Wall Street. The street was created in 1870 with the removal of the original city park during construction of the new depot. The Markham House stands at the end of the street along present Central Avenue. Built in 1875, the hotel was proud of its 105 sun-filled rooms, excusing two dark rooms as "adapted for railroad men and the night clerks who sleep in the daytime."

In 1875, the city dug an artesian well and constructed a water tank at the intersection of Peachtree, Marietta, and Decatur streets—now known as Five Points. Though this was an effort to ensure the city's water supply, it was never a reliable—or safe—source of city water. At this time, Edgewood Avenue had not yet been constructed from the Five Points area.

A shopper, carrying her store-wrapped package, crosses the hustle and bustle of busy Whitehall Street. In the distance beyond, a crowd fills the hectic intersection of the street, the rail line, and Peachtree Street farther on. The Kimball House rises in the background. The street here sloped downhill to the original surface grade of the railroad tracks before rising again along Peachtree Street.

In the years following the Civil War, Vinings Station became a popular destination for daylong pleasure trips to the countryside. Most people arrived by train and enjoyed not only the rustic charm of the crossroads town, but dancing and entertainment in the five pavilions built to attract the city's sightseers. An additional attraction was the distillery built here in the late 1860s by Rufus M. Rose, founder of the "Four Roses" whiskey blend.

By 1875, the Old St. Philip's church had grown to be the largest Episcopal congregation in the state, including the attendance of Federal officers and their families stationed in Atlanta during Reconstruction. The building was repaired from the heavy damage suffered in the war with their assistance, including appeals to northern friends and military band concerts. The church's new cathedral rises in the background.

A display of ladies' hats fills the windows and doorway of Julius Regenstein's millinery and dry goods store founded in 1872. Originally called the Surprise Store, Regenstein's offered everything a woman could desire and was supposedly the first store in the South to have a woman sales clerk.

Atlanta pioneer settlers Thomas W. Connally and his wife, Temperance Peacock, pose in front of their East Point home in 1883. The couple had 16 children. Standing with them is their granddaughter Electa, and their domestic servant, Aunt Martha. In the 1850s, the city of East Point, like Atlanta, developed around the terminus of a rail line, the Atlanta & West Point Railroad.

After the Kimball House burned in 1883, the hotel was rebuilt on its original site with the assistance of Hannibal I. Kimball, who then lived in Chicago. It reopened New Year's Day 1885, with 357 guest rooms, a 7-story atrium, 31 stores, and more than 20 public-event rooms. It was advertised as fireproof. In 1893, the owner, Hugh T. Inman, presented the Kimball House as a wedding gift to his daughter, Annie, and her husband, John W. Grant.

The Atlanta City Brewing Company was founded in 1867 at the corner of Harris and present Courtland streets as "City Brewery." When the wooden offices burned in 1880, a brick building was constructed directly over the existing storage cellars. During the 1880s, the firm brewed draught beer, delivered in barrels and kegs. At the same time, the company acquired an ice factory to supply its customers with free ice.

The fanlight of the Union Station train depot rises above a crowd waiting on President Grover Cleveland to emerge from his train car. Cleveland came to Atlanta in October 1887 to visit the Piedmont Exposition, the second of Atlanta's large fairs dedicated to southern manufacturing. The fair was organized by the Piedmont Exposition Company and was held on private grounds that now form the city's Piedmont Park.

The rustic, tented scenery in this albumen print is actually an ornate studio setting with a painted backdrop. Although the men's group is unidentified, the man seated second from right is Charles Hardy Ivy, a grandson of Atlanta pioneer Hardy Ivy. About 1833, the older Ivy built a log cabin on high ground near the corner of Courtland and Ellis streets. In doing so, he became the first white settler to build a home in what became downtown Atlanta.

A nursemaid and her wards stand before Christian Kontz's house along Marietta Street. As technology allowed photographers freedom to move out of the studio to document the American landscape, the homes of wealthy city residents became a favorite subject. Hired by the homeowners, photographers recorded residences as a confirmation of late-nineteenth-century American prosperity—complete with family members and domestics posed proudly, if sometimes awkwardly, in front.

In 1867, local officials proposed the city as Georgia's fifth state capital when a constitutional convention gathered in Atlanta. It was approved, but the question rose again in 1877, leading to a statewide referendum that selected Atlanta over Milledgeville as the permanent capital. In 1889, construction of the new $1 million capitol was completed on the site of Atlanta's antebellum city hall.

This panorama was taken from the dome of the new state capitol, facing northwest toward the heart of Atlanta in 1889. Just right of center is the barrel-vaulted roof of Union Station with the second Kimball House rising above it at the depot's north end. At lower-right are the cupola-topped Georgia Railroad Freight Depot and its long row of freight storage rooms running to the right edge.

Peachtree Street during the 1890s was full of grand homes shaded by tall, old trees. This view faces north along the street from the Ellis Street intersection. The house visible at left belonged to banker Robert H. Richards; the columned house next door is the Herring-Leyden House, occupied by Union general George H. Thomas during the Civil War. The Georgia Governor's Mansion stood just one block north at Cain and Peachtree streets.

Though West Peachtree Street in 1890 was a quiet residential neighborhood of middle-class homes, it had a busy existence during the 1880s. Until the mid 1870s, this had actually been the original course of Peachtree Street. It was not until the early 1880s that the street was fully extended to the present Pershing Point where it rejoins Peachtree Street. During the same period, the name was changed to Georgia Avenue, reverting to West Peachtree Street in 1885.

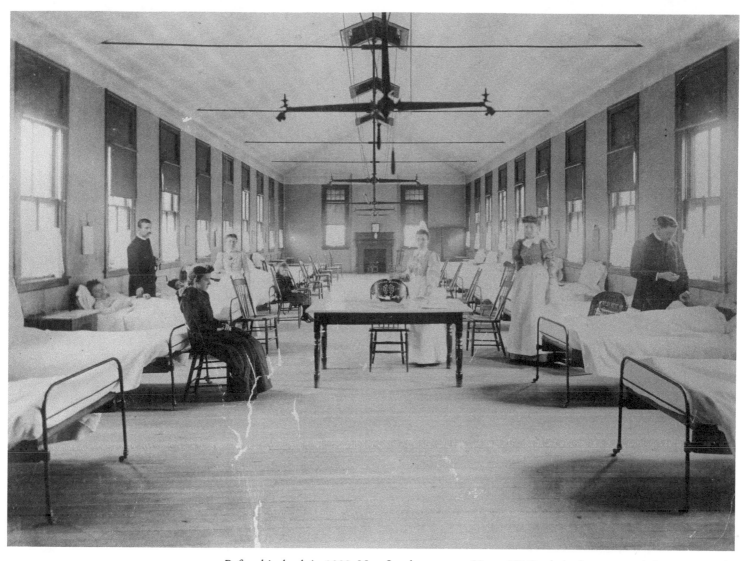

Before his death in 1889, New South promoter Henry W. Grady had encouraged the creation of a public hospital for Atlanta. In 1890, the year after his death, a hospital honoring him was approved by the city. In May 1892, Grady Memorial Hospital opened in its Butler Street building, providing one hundred beds in ten wards for patients. Today, Grady is the state's largest hospital, with nearly one million patient visits a year.

A group of bicyclists pose outside the home of William Bensel on Ellis Street. By the 1890s, "safety" bikes with a body frame and chain drive similar to modern bicycles provided both transportation and leisure. So many inexpensive, mass-produced bicycles were being devised and manufactured that the U.S. government maintained a separate patent office just for bicycles. Around the time of this photograph, Harry Dacre introduced his song "Daisy Bell (Give Me Your Answer True)"—also known as "A Bicycle Built for Two."

A new brougham sits on Ponce de Leon Avenue with horses Daisy and Dandy in harness. The coach has a front window, allowing occupants to see forward—here, the children of Clarence Knowles, Constance and Clarence, Jr. Knowles was president of the Piedmont Driving Club, founded to allow owners to display their horses and carriages on the club grounds, which became Piedmont Park. The names of the driver and nursemaid on the curb are not known.

The University of Georgia and Auburn University compete in the "Deep South's Oldest Rivalry" at present Piedmont Park in 1895. The Tigers won, 16–6. The schools' first football game was held in the park two years earlier, Auburn winning, 10–0. Georgia's coach was Glenn "Pop" Warner, who led the team to its first losing season at 3-4. The following year, the Bulldogs were co-champions of the Southern Intercollegiate Athletic Association with an undefeated, 4-0 record.

John Fritz stands on the back porch of his house along Piedmont Avenue north of present Tenth Street; his children, left to right, are Walter, Clara, Bertie, and Dolly, and family friend Albert McClure. Fritz opened a meat market in downtown Atlanta and maintained a cattle farm along the southern edge of present Piedmont Park. The cattle for his market grazed on leased property on what is now the park's Oak Hill area.

The Cotton States & International Exposition opened in 1895 as the third and largest of the city's fairs intended to promote the region's economy throughout the nation and the world. Creating facilities for the exposition included enlarging an existing lake into the present park's Clara Meer, whose name is laid out on the lake's bank. Family tradition maintains the lake was named in honor of Clara, John Fritz's young daughter who grew up on this land.

During the course of the three-month exposition, more than 800,000 attendees visited the grounds and buildings of the park. Public entertainment included motion pictures, at a public screening of the Phantascope, advertised as "Living Pictures." Admission was 25¢. In addition, guests were treated to a southern tradition, open-pit barbecue prepared on site. After the exposition, the buildings were removed and the grounds were purchased by the city, becoming Piedmont Park.

SHOOTING THE CHUTES

256

To publicize the southern economy, the exposition included displays of agriculture, industry, and manufacturing, as well as buildings dedicated to the achievement of both women and African Americans. Visitors to the exposition included former President Grover Cleveland, Booker T. Washington, who delivered his "Atlanta Compromise" speech, and John Philip Sousa, who composed his "King Cotton" march for the fair. Recreation included a midway with Ferris wheel, a Wild West show, and the "Shoot the Chutes."

Women workers, including children, take a break for a company photograph at the Marsh and Smith pants factory. The production of ready-to-wear men's clothing increased throughout the nineteenth century, along with the growth of the southern textile industry and availability of women employees. Edward Marsh and John Smith ran their dry goods store offering boots and shoes along with their pants manufactory in the mid-1890s at the corner of Pryor Street and Edgewood Avenue.

Gentlemen lodgers pose in front of their rooming house, which they designated the "Skull and Crossbones Boarding House." Family homes such as this were normally run by a landlady, who provided inexpensive room and board for single men and women. In the case of the Skull and Crossbones, two men shared each of the four available rooms. In certain ways, the boardinghouse concept lives on in the modern Bed and Breakfast.

Customers meet and talk while inspecting curbside stalls constructed at the edge of the rail line next to the second Kimball House. By the end of the nineteenth century, an emergent African American middle class was involved in Atlanta's black educational institutions as well as in diversifying positions in business, trades, and services. In 1900, the city directory began publishing a separate listing for black residents, who composed 40 percent of the city's population.

A laborer unloads coal along Edgewood Avenue a few years after the street was created. When developer Joel Hurt organized the Atlanta and Edgewood Street Railroad Company, he intended it to provide direct service from downtown Atlanta to the Inman Park suburb. When the company was chartered in 1886, however, the street did not exist. Only a short alley and some of these buildings existed there. Within a few years, Hurt bought the necessary right-of-way and opened the city's first electric trolley line.

Men pose on a Courtland & Washington street railway car as they would have ridden: whites seated in the front and blacks in the back. Between 1900 and 1906, African Americans in many southern cities, including Atlanta and Augusta, Georgia, and Montgomery, Alabama, organized boycotts of segregated streetcars. The boycotts took place during a period of growing racial tension, culminating in Atlanta in the 1906 Race Riot.

Symbols of the city's old and new, Atlanta's future electric railway system is under construction below the skeleton of the city's abandoned artesian well at today's Five Points intersection. As the nineteenth century drew to a close, the bustling business town had recovered from the destruction of the Civil War and grown into the self-proclaimed capital of Henry Grady's New South, promoting itself as the commercial and financial center of a changing southern economy.

Forward Atlanta: From Boomtown to Southern Symbol

(1900–1939)

Shoppers on foot and in buggy pass along Whitehall Street beneath the recently completed Century Building at the Alabama Street intersection. At the turn of the century, Atlanta's population was 90,000, making it the largest city in the state and the third-largest in the Southeast. Residents included a large number of African Americans, drawn to the city by opportunities for employment and for its educational institutions, including Atlanta University and Spelman College.

The Georgia State Capitol rises above central Atlanta, towering over area churches, hotels, and buildings associated with the downtown railroads. In late 1900, however, efforts began to replace the city's old Union Station, now almost 30 years old. Within a few years, Atlanta would no longer converge around the Zero-Mile post that marked the city's founding. New stations, the automobile, and the airplane would transform the terminal city into a new sort of transportation center.

By 1901, there were only two remaining street railway systems in the city: Atlanta Rapid Transit Company and the Atlanta Consolidated Street Railway Company. The resulting competition between the two—dubbed the Second Battle of Atlanta—was severe, resulting in fare wars, court injunctions, and meetings to plan battle strategies. Ultimately, the mayor and city council approved an ordinance permitting the two companies to consolidate, thus creating the Georgia Railway & Electric Company.

Maxwell Berry's garden gives an indication of the appearance of upper-class homes shortly after the turn of the century, including a well, smokehouse, and stable for one horse. Berry was a contractor who built both Kimball houses, the Church of the Immaculate Conception, Trinity Methodist Church, First Presbyterian Church, and the U.S. Post Office and Customs House. During the Civil War, his ten-year-old daughter, Carrie, kept a diary of the siege of Atlanta.

Franklyn Howland poses at left with his brother, Leroy. Between 1904 and 1906, Franklyn's wife, Anne, kept a trip log for another car, his red Cadillac Runabout. In her first entry, July 31, she writes: "We started from the Kimball House at 9 a.m. Road fair. Every blooming horse & team we met was 'skeered' into fits & but for the courtesy of our chauffeur the road would have been full of broken teams & mashed women & babies."

A familiar question in the history of photography is, Why didn't people ever smile in old pictures? With the advent of amateur snapshots like this one, the formality of the professional photographer's studio no longer inhibited the person whose picture was being taken. This group, photographed out-of-doors by a friend, feels at ease to pose in jest in an area lumberyard.

Crowds line downtown Atlanta streets as President Theodore Roosevelt, standing in his carriage, passes up Peachtree Street in October 1905. The parade took an hour to work its way to Piedmont Park, where Roosevelt spoke to a crowd of thousands. Roosevelt then toured parts of the city before giving a speech to students at Georgia Tech. While he was in Atlanta, Roosevelt also visited his mother's family home, Bulloch Hall, in Roswell.

Unfortunately, the photographer of this exceptional portrait of five women in succeeding generations of the same family is unknown. Yet it is a simple and elegant image in which the individual personality of each is clearly conveyed. Left to right are Julia Ann Hollingsworth (Stewart), Bobbie Jones (McClain), Allie Frances Walters, Frances McClain (Walters), and Sarah Elizabeth Stewart (Jones).

In 1883, the city accepted 100 acres offered by businessman Lemuel P. Grant for a park southeast of downtown. Named Grant Park in his honor, it remains the city's oldest public park. The park included Lake Abana, popular for scenic boat rides. It was expanded in 1906 but drained in the 1960s. The park is home to the present Zoo Atlanta and the Cyclorama, a circular painting depicting the Battle of Atlanta.

Charles Golden stands at the entrance to his meat market and home, located on Marietta Street at Ponders Avenue. Meat sanitation was a concern in early Atlanta and in 1853 slaughterhouses were removed to beyond the city limits, which at that time was near Golden's future butcher shop. By 1905, city residents had a wide variety of grocers from whom to choose, as well as specialty vendors for meats, fruits, milk, fish and oysters, and coffee roasts.

Dorsey's Grocery stood at the corner of Peachtree and East Paces Ferry roads in the heart of today's Buckhead neighborhood. Robert Dorsey provided delivery services throughout the area in the buggy at right, but closed his store around 1907 because of unpaid bills. In 1841, the first post office had come to the area, named Irbyville for Henry Irby, owner of a tavern that once had a buck's head mounted on a post.

Opening in 1905, Terminal Station offered service via Southern Railway, Seaboard Air Line, Central of Georgia, and the Atlanta and West Point railroads. The building, located at Mitchell and present Spring streets, was planned by architect P. Thornton Marye, who also designed the Fox Theatre. The station served Atlanta for more than 60 years until it was demolished in 1972. By that time, air travel had replaced the city's rail lines as the primary mode of transportation in the Southeast.

An interior panorama shows employees and customers of the Fielder & Allen office supply company on Marietta Street in 1908. Over the next few decades, founder Ivan E. Allen became a leading civic booster, writing frequently in the newspapers, organizing public fund-raisers, and serving as president of the Atlanta Chamber of Commerce. In 1919, the company changed names to the Ivan Allen–Marshall Company and became the Ivan Allen Company in 1953.

An automobile full of sightseers from the city pulls along a dirt street in rural Dunwoody in 1911. This area of DeKalb County had been partitioned for settlement following the first Treaty of Indian Springs, signed with the Creeks in 1821. Between 1805 and 1832, the state redistributed tribal property through a lottery; this area was awarded to settlers through a lottery held the same year the treaty was signed.

Before the arrival of settlers to the area, this was the intersection of two important trading routes of the Creek confederacy. The Peachtree Trail, which began in northeast Georgia, ended here; Peachtree Road was built along a section of this trail during the War of 1812. The Sandtown Trail ran between Stone Mountain and the Creek settlement of Sandtown on the Chattahoochee River. Today's Cascade Road in southwest Atlanta follows the route of the Indian trail.

Completed in 1897, the Flatiron Building is Atlanta's oldest surviving steel-framed skyscraper, rising 11 stories above Broad and Peachtree streets. It was designed by Bradford Gilbert and is officially named the English-American Building for the English-American Loan and Trust Company for which it was built. It was labeled "flatiron" after New York City's famous Flatiron skyscraper, which was actually constructed five years after Atlanta's building.

A group of Gideons poses with Bibles in front of the second Kimball House before delivering them to city hotels. Founded in 1899, Gideons International began distributing free Bibles in 1908 and had placed more than one million Bibles in hotel rooms within 20 years.

This lighthearted group, with guns pointed at each other and the viewer, are out for a drive and picture-taking near Chamblee on Christmas Day 1910. The City of Chamblee had been incorporated only two years earlier, and the surrounding countryside, though home to pastures for the local dairy farms, was still heavily wooded.

Although snow is rare in Atlanta's climate, it creates a white wonderland after the first fall, as here in 1914. Unfortunately, it also brings the city to a standstill when it arrives, especially when it includes ice. Atlanta was paralyzed for several days in February 1905 by the heaviest snow and ice storm on record up to that time. The city again stopped when an unpredicted storm, dubbed "Snow Jam," hit Atlanta in January 1982, stranding thousands of commuters.

Union Station continued to serve the city even after the opening of Terminal Station a few years earlier. This image, recorded from the vantage of the Peachtree Street viaduct in 1914, gives a strong impression of the area dubbed the "train gulch." Enclosed by the surrounding buildings, including the Kimball House at left, the old rail depot was a center of smoke and noise.

City day-trippers pose along the climb to the top of Stone Mountain, referred to on early maps of the region as Rock Mountain. The dome of the mountain, formed 300 million years ago, is the largest exposed granite outcrop in the world. Once owned by the Venable family, the mountain is now part of a state park that offers a cable car to the top and the same trail used by these sightseers.

Firemen pose with their horse-drawn and horse-less equipment in front of Fire Station No. 11 on North Avenue in Midtown. The station opened in 1909 and was listed on the National Register of Historic Places in 1980. It still stands after reopening as a restaurant in 2003.

Inman Park was the city's first suburban community, developed by businessman Joel Hurt between 1885 and 1889 two miles east of the central business district. Planning for the 90-acre neighborhood included 10 acres set aside for Springvale Park, including Crystal Lake, located in the center of the community. It was at this time that Hurt also constructed Edgewood Avenue and the street's railway running in a direct line from downtown to the Inman Park Trolley Barn.

Following U.S. entry into World War I, a site near Chamblee along the Southern Railway was selected for a new training camp, named Camp Gordon. By the middle of the summer tents had appeared, and as the *Atlanta Journal* reported, "Cornfields have given way to barracks that will shelter Uncle Sam's fighting men, roads have been cut through hills, spurs of railroad track have been laid, trees have been felled to make way for barracks and mess halls . . ."

Born a slave, Alonzo F. Herndon (standing behind the word "Atlanta" in the banner) owned a series of barbershops in the city, becoming Atlanta's wealthiest African American at his death in 1927. In 1905, he founded the basis of the Atlanta Life Insurance Company, which when this photograph was taken had become one of the nation's largest African American insurance companies. Herndon was a leader in the civic life of the community, supporting education, orphanages, the Y.M.C.A., and local churches.

The Henry Grady Hotel appears at center above Peachtree Street in this image facing south toward today's Margaret Mitchell Square. Peachtree Plaza, which opened in 1976 as the world's tallest hotel, now rises on the site. To the left is the Davison-Paxon department store constructed in 1924, whose building housed the downtown Macy's at the end of the twentieth century. Beyond is the Winecoff Hotel, site of the nation's deadliest hotel fire in 1946.

As businesses expanded north along Peachtree Street, the once-grand homes of the city's elite were adapted to commercial use. By the mid-1920s, this home had been converted to the Hotel Adair after serving as home to Miss Ballard's Seminary and other business firms. A one-story arcade of small shops has been erected along what would once have been the home's orderly front yard.

As early as 1912, the United Daughters of the Confederacy had supported the idea of a memorial carved into the side of Stone Mountain. Within a few years, a memorial association commissioned Gutzon Borglum to carve the proposed sculpture depicting Robert E. Lee, Jefferson Davis, and Thomas J. "Stonewall" Jackson. Work began in 1923 and General Lee's head was unveiled on Lee's birthday in 1924.

In 1925, Gutzon Borglum left the Confederate memorial project; he later executed the sculptures at Mt. Rushmore, from 1927 to 1941. A second sculptor, Augustus Lukeman, resumed work at Stone Mountain in 1925 by removing previous carving, only to abandon the project in 1928 when funding and a 12-year deadline ran out. The carving remained unfinished until 1964, when work resumed under state sponsorship. Following a dedication ceremony in 1970, the last details were completed in 1972.

Cheerleaders and fans pose during an Atlanta University football game with Clark University in the mid-1920s. Atlanta University was founded in 1865 by the American Missionary Association. After its first classes were held in a railroad boxcar, the university acquired 60 acres on Atlanta's west side with funds from the Freedman's Bureau. In 1929, the university discontinued undergraduate work and united with Morehouse and Spelman colleges as the Atlanta University System.

Clark University was founded in 1869 as the Summer Hill School by the Freedman's Aid Society of
the Methodist Church. The school later moved to a campus at Whitehall and McDaniel streets and
was chartered as Clark University in 1877. In 1941, the university was renamed Clark College and
relocated to its present site adjoining Atlanta University. In 1988, the two football rivals merged into
the present Clark Atlanta University.

Among the many subjects photojournalist Tracy Mathewson documented were the cultural traditions of Atlanta and the South, from religious baptism to political barbecues. The location of this baptism is unknown, but it would have taken place in the countryside near the city.

Tracy Mathewson was Atlanta's first professional news photojournalist, working for the *Atlanta Georgian* and other local newspapers beginning in the 1910s. As a photojournalist, his still photographs and newsreels covered a rich variety of topics, including the Atlanta fire of 1917 as well as sports figures, city and state politicians, sporting events, and church baptisms.

Forsyth Street appears dark and unfriendly as the Great Depression begins in 1929, but the decade had been good to Atlanta. The city's "Forward Atlanta" campaign had created 20,000 jobs valued at $34.5 million to the local economy. Although the economy slowed during the 1930s, some innovative components were developed, including the new airport, Candler Field. Although Candler eventually supplanted the rail lines that had formed the city, it secured Atlanta's future as a transportation center.

Atlanta in 1930 is dominated by the rail lines with Terminal Station at lower-right. Crossing horizontally across the rail lines is the city's largest civic project of the foregoing decade—the Spring Street Viaduct. At a cost of $1 million, the overpass was part of a long-range plan to construct bridges or "viaducts" spanning the rail lines to ease crosstown traffic. The process resulted in Underground Atlanta as streetscapes were raised one floor to match the viaduct's level.

The Paramount Theater at today's Margaret Mitchell Square opened in 1920 as the Howard Theater, designed by Hentz, Reid, and Adler, one of the city's most prestigious architectural firms. When the theater closed and was demolished in 1960, the front elevation was saved and reused as the facade of a residence. The theater stood next to Loew's Grand (the former DeGive Opera House) where *Gone With the Wind* premiered in 1939.

Like something out of a Marx Brothers comedy, students at the Ivy Street School dress as cavemen for a class event. Atlanta had established a public school system in 1872, yet by the turn of the century only about 50 percent of the youth attended classes. Reforms in the 1920s, including a compulsory attendance law, free textbooks, and enforced child-labor regulations, resulted in 90 percent attendance by the end of the 1930s.

The William Oliver Building—named for sons William and Oliver Healey of the original owner—remains an example of Art Deco architecture as part of the Fairlie-Poplar Historic District in downtown Atlanta. Bounded by Marietta, Peachtree, Luckie, and Cone streets, the district holds a variety of architecture, including Renaissance Revival, Neoclassical, Georgian Revival, and Victorian styles.

On February 22, 1930, city records were moved to Atlanta's new neo-Gothic City Hall at Washington and Mitchell streets. The building was erected on the site of Girls' High School, property which included the Neal-Lyon House that had served as General Sherman's headquarters during the Civil War. The building is Atlanta's fourth city hall. The main city offices remained here until a new addition on Trinity Street opened in 1989.

Atlanta's Fox Theatre opened Christmas Day 1929, just as the Roaring Twenties came to a close. Originally built as the Yaarab Temple Shrine Mosque, the theater declared bankruptcy less than one year after opening. Despite success in the 1940s, audiences decreased in the following decades until corporate interests sought to demolish the building in the 1970s. Saved through a preservation campaign, the Fox remains home to films, ballet, theatrical productions, and other cultural events.

Crowds gather outside the city's third Union Station, opened in 1930, to hear President Franklin
D. Roosevelt. The depot was built above the tracks along the Forsyth Street viaduct rather than at
ground level. It marked another crossroads in transportation, ending nearly eight decades in which
the old depot had been the city center. "Feet that for generations have worn a path to the old station,"
remarked the newspaper, "will beat another to the new."

This model home on former Chestnut Street near Simpson Street was procured and remodeled by the construction firm of Walter H. "Chief" Aiken in 1936. Aiken, former football coach of Atlanta University, was a leading civic and business leader in Atlanta's African American community. During the Great Depression, Aiken remodeled this home to show what could be done to improve property through tax-dollar assistance from the Federal Housing Authority.

President Franklin D. Roosevelt speaks at Georgia Tech's Grant Field during the dedication ceremony for Techwood Homes, the nation's first public housing project. In 1935, the New Deal sponsored two urban renewal projects in the city, Techwood Homes for whites and University Homes for blacks. The latter project was a collaborative effort between Atlanta real estate developer Charles Palmer and John Hope, president of Atlanta University.

In September 1926, the first air mail flight left Atlanta for Macon, Jacksonville, Tampa, Fort Myers, and Miami. Passenger service from Atlanta to Dallas and Los Angeles was inaugurated in October 1930 with service by American Airlines. By the end of 1930, only New York and Chicago had more regularly scheduled flights than Atlanta's Candler Field. Sixteen planes a day were arriving and departing, carrying mail, express, and passengers.

The nation's first air-traffic control tower opened at Candler Field in March 1939. During World War II, the airport doubled in size and set a record with 1,700 departures and arrivals in a single day, making it the nation's busiest airport for flight operations. In 1946, Candler Field was renamed Atlanta Municipal Airport, and two years later, more than one million passengers passed through its terminal.

Atlanta Constitution photojournalist Kenneth G. Rogers took this view of snow-covered track in downtown Atlanta after an ice storm. The tracks in the foreground lead from the new Union Station depot at Forsyth Street. Working for the newspaper for more than 50 years, Rogers served as the head of photography for the paper's magazine, earning the title "dean of southern photographers."

One of the city's most tragic fires erupted in November 1936, when a blaze gutted the Cable Piano Company building on Broad Street. The fire resulted in six deaths, and another six persons jumped from the building. A subsequent investigation determined the city fire department lacked adequate equipment, including aerial ladders and smoke masks. In addition to fire-fighting equipment, fire fighters needed less crowded conditions, which had resulted in "mob hysteria" at the scene.

On December 15, 1939, the motion picture version of Margaret Mitchell's Pulitzer Prize–winning novel, *Gone With the Wind,* premiered at Loew's Grand Theater. The movie release only added to the legend surrounding the book, its characters, and the author. As the 1930s drew to a close, Atlanta, Peachtree Street, and Scarlett O'Hara had entered the public imagination as symbols of the American South.

Flanked by Olivia de Havilland and Laurence Olivier, the film's star, Vivien Leigh, sips champagne at a press party held at the Georgian Terrace Hotel. Following the premiere of *Gone With the Wind,* the actors attended a breakfast complete with southern dishes, including ham, biscuits, and hominy. By 8:00 A.M., they had all departed by plane for Hollywood and by train to New York.

The movie version of *Gone With the Wind* was filmed almost entirely in California. Both Clark Gable and Vivien Leigh, therefore, participated in a number of events intended to introduce them to Atlanta and the South. The pair toured columned southern mansions and visited the Cyclorama painting depicting the Battle of Atlanta, where Gable was introduced to a miniature figure with his likeness that had been added to the diorama.

White boaters and white shoes were the fashion of the day in 1940s downtown Atlanta. During the decade, a once-familiar sound throughout the city would disappear—the grinding, screeching sound of the steel-wheeled railway car against metal rails.

CENTENNIAL CITY: FROM SOUTHERN METROPOLIS TO OLYMPIC VILLAGE

(1940–1996)

Coming north from the original depot site, the intersection of Peachtree and Forsyth streets with the present Park Place is the point where Peachtree Street turned north to follow a ridge line that is a geological drainage-basin divide. Since Atlanta sits along the Eastern Continental Divide, rainwater falling on the east side of the divide runs into the Atlantic Ocean while rainwater on the west side runs into the Gulf of Mexico.

A streetcar turns the bend on Peachtree Street at West Peachtree and Baker streets. In 1886, Jefferson Davis dedicated a monument to Georgia senator Benjamin H. Hill that stood in a small park here. The statue was later moved to protect it from vandals and the "inevitable and ubiquitous initial carvers," in the words of city historian Franklin Garrett. In 1912, the grade of Peachtree Street was lowered, leveling the descent into West Peachtree Street and clearing the park for business development.

The columned entrance to the Hurt Building appears at left, located on the site of the car barn for the mule-drawn railway. The building was constructed from 1913 to 1926 in a triangular V-shape similar to other Atlanta skyscrapers, including the nearby Candler Building. Businessman Joel Hurt planned the building before hiring J. E. R. Carpenter, a New York architect experienced in high-rise designs, to complete the final plans.

Bell Bomber workers, 37 percent of them women, manufactured more than 600 airplanes during World War II at the Bell Aircraft plant in Marietta. Although the plant closed following the end of the war, it was reopened in 1952 by the Lockheed Corporation. The federal government's investment in war industries in Atlanta during World War II had a dramatic impact on the area's future economy.

Buses, automobiles, and streetcars let passengers out in front of Davison-Paxon's department store at Peachtree and Ellis streets. Atlanta has always been a shopping destination with important local retail stores including Rich's, Davison's, J. P. Allen, Regenstein's, and George Muse's clothing company. All of these establishments maintained a flagship store in downtown Atlanta. Today, Atlanta remains a regional retail center with shopping malls such as Lenox Square and Phipps Plaza.

The Winecoff Hotel was considered the finest in the city when it opened in 1913. Advertised as "fireproof," it nevertheless had no fire alarms, fire escapes, or sprinkler system. On December 7, 1946, the hotel was filled almost to capacity when a fire began around 3:00 A.M. With the loss of 119 people, it remains the deadliest hotel fire in U.S. history. The building still stands at the corner of Peachtree and Ellis streets.

The message "Jesus Saves" rises over Auburn Avenue on the Big Bethel AME Church in the historic African American neighborhood called "Sweet Auburn." The street became the center of the city's black social, political, economic, and religious life in the 1930s. Other significant buildings include Ebenezer Baptist Church, where Martin Luther King, Jr., was pastor; the Royal Peacock club, headlining B. B. King and Gladys Knight; and the Atlanta Life Insurance Company, founded by Alonzo Herndon.

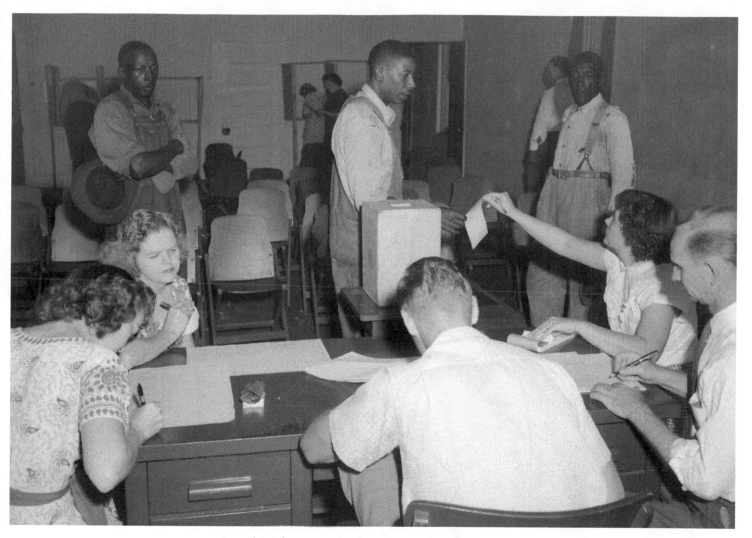

In 1945, Atlanta contained approximately 3,000 registered African American voters. The following year, the All-Citizens Registration Committee registered almost 18,000 new black voters in less than two months. The committee was a coalition of representatives of the National Association for the Advancement of Colored People (NAACP), the Urban League, the Atlanta Civic and Political League, and other black organizations. Though still a minority, the African American community enjoyed growing electoral strength because of such efforts.

Newspaper reporters, photographers, and managers moved into the new offices of the *Atlanta Constitution* on December 26, 1947. The newspaper was founded in 1868 and at one time or another included Henry W. Grady, Joel Chandler Harris, and Margaret Mitchell as staff writers. Around 1890, the newspaper had the widest geographic distribution in the nation. The building was designed by Robert & Company with relief sculpture by Julian Harris, who executed sculpture for 52 public buildings in the Southeast.

Plaza Park, dedicated in August 1949, was a modernist island amid the remnants of the past. To its right is the second Kimball House, built in 1885, and unlike its neighbor, the small urban park existed only briefly. The area has become the plaza entrance to Underground Atlanta, where a giant peach is dropped at midnight on New Year's Eve.

In June 1904, the city purchased the property of the Cotton States & International Exposition, creating Piedmont Park. A few years later, the city hired Olmsted Brothers to create a master design plan for developing the park; though that plan was never fully realized, it created a vision for the future. Today, the park serves as the venue for the Atlanta Pride Festival, the Montreux Jazz Festival, and the Atlanta Dogwood Festival.

Fireworks explode over Lakewood Park, site of the annual Southeastern Fair located on the grounds of the original city waterworks. From 1916 to 1978, the fair was often the state's largest attraction, with displays of livestock, agriculture, art, and farm machinery, horse and auto racing, a midway, and a fireworks show.

The view from the grandstand at Ponce de Leon ballpark in April 1949 included a magnolia tree just right of center field. The home of the Crackers, it was commonly called "Poncey" and was the only stadium allowing for a tree—462 feet from home plate—in the outfield. If a ball was hit into the giant magnolia, it was in play. In 1966, after Atlanta-Fulton County Stadium was built, the ballpark was taken down. The magnolia tree still stands.

Spelman College, blanketed in snow, was founded as the Atlanta Baptist Female Seminary by Sophia B. Packard and Harriet E. Giles in 1881. With support from John D. Rockefeller, the school located to its current site in 1884 and was named Spelman Seminary in honor of Harvey and Lucy Spelman, the abolitionist parents of Rockefeller's wife, Laura. Spelman College is the nation's oldest historically black college for women and is a member of the Atlanta University Center.

In 1901, the Atlanta Steel Hoop Company was founded to manufacture barrel hoops and cotton bale ties. The company changed its name to Atlantic Steel in 1915 and expanded its product line to include barbed wire, fence posts, rails, and nails. The company also expanded geographically to encompass a 140-acre industrial site just north of the Georgia Tech campus. The property has now been redeveloped as a mixed-use community, Atlantic Station.

With paper icicles hanging in the windows, Atlanta's first air-conditioned (trackless) trolley offers a cool ride on the East Point–to–Hapeville line. Following World War II, transit use fell as electric trolleys were replaced with buses. In an effort to attract riders, the system tried cool comfort and—descending the front steps—a bus stewardess. Around the same time, the seasonal highest demands on the power company's electricity generation switched from winter to summer as southerners embraced air conditioning.

The Peachtree Arcade is packed with shoppers and visitors listening to evangelist Billy Graham, who is standing on the mezzanine stairs during a noontime prayer. The arcade was built in 1917, providing an enclosed shopping mall, restaurants, and entertainment one block south of Five Points.

Mayor Ivan Allen, Jr., sought to bring major league sports teams to Atlanta and in anticipation of relocating the Milwaukee Braves, the city approved construction of Atlanta–Fulton County Stadium, completed in 1965. Allen later stated they had built a stadium on "land we didn't own, with money we didn't have, for teams that didn't exist." Home to the Atlanta Braves baseball team and the Atlanta Falcons football team for many years, it was razed in 1997 following the Centennial Olympic Games, held in the city in 1996.

Notes on the Photographs

These notes, listed by page number, attempt to include all aspects known of the photographs. Each of the photographs is identified by the page number, a title or description, photographer and collection, archive, and call or box number when applicable. Although every attempt was made to collect all data, in some cases complete data may have been unavailable due to the age and condition of some of the photographs and records.

Printed in the USA
CPSIA information can be obtained
at www.ICGtesting.com
JSHW072023140824
68134JS00042B/3755